THE COLLABORATORS

Robert Hichens

[ZHINGOORA BOOKS]

This edition is published by
Zhingoora Books.

Contents

I.

"Why shouldn't we collaborate?" said Henley in his most matter-of-fact way, as Big Ben gave voice to the midnight hour. "Everybody does it nowadays. Two heads may be really better than one, although I seldom believe in the truth of accepted sayings. Your head is a deuced good one, Andrew; but—now don't get angry—you are too excitable and too intense to be left quite to yourself, even in book-writing, much less in the ordinary affairs of life. I think you were born to collaborate, and to collaborate with me. You can give me everything I lack, and I can give you a little of the sense of humour, and act as a drag upon the wheel."

"None of the new humour, Jack; that shall never appear in a book with my name attached to it. Dickens I can tolerate. He is occasionally felicitous. The story of 'The Dying Clown,' for instance, crude as it is it has a certain grim tragedy about it. But the new humour came from the pit, and should go—to the *Sporting Times*."

"Now, don't get excited. The book is not in proof yet—perhaps never will be. You need not be afraid. My humour will probably be old enough. But what do you y to the idea?"

Andrew Trenchard sat for awhile in silent consideration. His legs were stretched out, and his slippered feet rested on the edge of the brass fender. A nimbus of smoke surrounded his swarthy features, his shock of black hair, his large, rather morose, dark eyes. He was a man of about twenty-five, with an almost horribly intelligent face, so observant that he tried people, so acute that he frightened them. His intellect was never for a moment at rest, unless in sleep. He devoured himself with his own emotions, and others with his analysis of theirs. His mind was always crouching to spring, except when it was springing. He lived an irregular life, and all horrors had a subtle fascination for him. As Henley had remarked, he possessed little sense of humour, but immense sense of evil and tragedy and sorrow. He seldom found time to calmly regard the drama of life from the front. He was always at the stage-door, sending in his card, and requesting admittance behind the scenes. What was on the surface only interested him in so far as it indicated what was beneath, and in all mental matters his normal procedure was that of the disguised detective. Stupid people disliked him. Clever people distrusted him while they admired him. The mediocre suggested that he was liable to go off his head, and the profound predicted for him fame, tempered by suicide.

Most people considered him interesting, and a few were sincerely attached to him. Among these last was Henley, who had been his friend at Oxford, and had taken rooms in the same house with him in Smith's Square, Westminster. Both the young men were journalists. Henley, who, as he had acknowledged, possessed a keen sense of humour, and was not so much ashamed of it as he ought to have been, wrote—very occasionally—for *Punch*, and more often for *Fun*, was dramatic critic of a lively society paper, and "did" the books—in a sarcastic vein—for a very unmuzzled "weekly," that was libellous by profession and truthful by oversight. Trenchard, on the other hand, wrote a good deal of very condensed fiction, and generally placed it; contributed brilliant fugitive articles to various papers and magazines, and was generally spoken of by the inner circle of the craft as "a rising man," and a man to be afraid of. Henley was full of common-sense, only moderately introspective, facile, and vivacious. He might be trusted to tincture a book with the popular element, and yet not to spoil it; for his literary sense was keen, despite his jocular leaning toward the new humour. He lacked imagination; but his descriptive powers were racy, and he knew instinctively what was likely to take, and what would be caviare to the general.

Trenchard, as he considered the proposition now made to him, realized that Henley might supply much that he lacked in any book that was written with a view to popular success. There could be no doubt of it.

"But we should quarrel inevitably and doggedly," he said at last. "If I can not hold myself in, still less can I be held in. We should tear one another in pieces. When I write, I feel that what I write must be, however crude, however improper or horrible it may seem. You would want to hold me back."

"My dear boy, I should more than want to—I should do it. In collaboration, no man can be a law unto himself. That must be distinctly understood before we begin. I don't wish to force the proposition on you. Only we are both ambitious devils. We are both poor. We are both determined to try a book. Have we more chance of succeeding if we try one together? I believe so. You have the imagination, the grip, the stern power to evolve the story, to make it seem inevitable, to force it step by step on its way. I can lighten that way. I can plant a few flowers—they shall not be peonies, I promise you—on the roadside. And I can, and, what is more, will, check you when you wish to make the story impossibly horrible or fantastic to the verge of the insane. Now, you needn't be angry. This book, if we write it, has got to be a good book, and yet a book that will bring grist to the mill. That is understood."

Andrew's great eyes flashed in the lamplight.

"The mill," he said. "Sometimes I feel inclined to let it stop working. Who would care if one wheel ceased to turn? There are so many others."

"Ah, that's the sort of thing I shall cut out of the book!" cried Henley, turning the soda-water into his whisky with a cheerful swish.

"We will be powerful, but never morbid; tragic, if you like, but not without hope. We need not aspire too much; but we will not look at the stones in the road all the time. And the dunghills, in which those weird fowl, the pessimistic realists, love to rake, we will sedulously avoid. Cheer up, old fellow, and be thankful that you possess a corrective in me."

Trenchard's face lightened in a rare smile as, with a half-sigh, he said:

"I believe you are right, and that I need a collaborator, an opposite, who is yet in sympathy with me. Yes; either of us might fail alone; together we should succeed."

"*Will* succeed, my boy!"

"But not by pandering to the popular taste," added Andrew in his most sombre tones, and with a curl of his thin, delicately-moulded lips. "I shall never consent to that."

"We will not call it pandering. But we must hit the taste of the day, or we shall look a couple of fools."

"People are always supposed to look fools when, for once, they are not fools," said Andrew.

"Possibly. But now our bargain is made. Strike hands upon it. Henceforth we are collaborators as well as friends."

Andrew extended his long, thin, feverish hand, and, as Henley held it for a moment, he started at the intense, vivid, abnormal personality its grasp seemed to reveal. To collaborate with Trenchard was to collaborate with a human volcano.

"And now for the germ of our book," he said, as the clock struck one. "Where shall we find it?"

Trenchard leaned forward in his chair, with his hands pressed upon the arms.

"Listen, and I will give it you," he said.

And, almost until the dawn and the wakening of the slumbering city, Henley sat and listened, and forgot that his pipe was smoked out, and that his feet were cold. Trenchard had strange powers, and could enthral as he could also repel.

"It is a weird idea, and it is very powerful," Henley said at last. "But you stop short at the critical moment. Have you not devised a *dénouement?*"

"Not yet. That is where the collaboration will come in. You must help me. We must talk it over. I am in doubt."

He got up and passed his hands nervously through his thick hair.

"My doubt has kept me awake so many nights!" he said, and his voice was rather husky and worn.

Henley looked at him almost compassionately.

"How intensely you live in your fancies!"

"My fancies?" said Andrew, with a sudden harsh accent, and darting a glance of curious watchfulness upon his friend. "My—— Yes, yes. Perhaps I do. Perhaps I try to. Some people have souls that must escape from their environment, their miserable life-envelope, or faint. Many of us labour and produce merely to create an atmosphere in which we ourselves may breathe for awhile and be happy. Damn this London, and this lodging, and this buying bread with words! I must create for myself an atmosphere. I must be always getting away from what is, even if I go lower, lower. Ah! Well—but the *dénouement*. Give me your impressions."

Henley meditated for awhile. Then he said; "Let us leave it. Let us get to work; and in time, as the story progresses, it will seem inevitable. We shall see it in front of us, and we shall not be able to avoid it. Let us get to work"—he glanced at his watch and laughed—"or, rather, let us get to bed. It is past four. This way madness lies. When we collaborate, we will write in the morning. Our book shall be a book of the dawn, and not of the darkness, despite its sombre theme."

"No, no; it must be a book of the darkness."

"Of the darkness, then, but written in the dawn. Your tragedy tempered by my trust in human nature, and the power that causes things to right themselves. Good-night, old boy."

"Good-night."

When Henley had left the room, Tren-chard sat for a moment with his head sunk low on his breast and his eyes half closed. Then, with a jerk, he gained his feet, went to the door, opened it, and looked forth on the deserted landing. He listened, and heard

Henley moving to and fro in his bedroom. Then he shut the door, took off his smoking-coat, and bared his left arm. There was a tiny blue mark on it.

"What will the *dénouement* be?" he whispered to himself, as he felt in his waistcoat pocket with a trembling hand.

II.

The book was moving onward by slow degrees and with a great deal of discussion.

In those days Henley and Trenchard lived much with sported oaks. They were battling for fame. They were doing all they knew. Literary gatherings missed them. First nights knew them no more. The grim intensity that was always characteristic of Trenchard seemed in some degree communicated to Henley. He began to more fully understand what the creating for one's self of an atmosphere meant. The story he and his friend were fashioning fastened upon him like some strange, determined shadow from the realms of real life, gripped him more and more closely, held him for long spells of time in a new and desolate world. For the book so far was a deepening tragedy, and although, at times, Henley strove to resist the paramount influence which the genius of Trenchard began to exercise over him, he found himself comparatively impotent, unable to shed gleams of popular light upon the darkness of the pages. The power of the tale was undoubted. Henley felt that it was a big thing that they two were doing; but would it be a popular thing—a money-making thing? That was the question. He sometimes wished with all his heart they had chosen a different subject to work their combined talent upon. The germ of the work seemed only capable of tragic treatment, if the book were to be artistic. Their hero was a man of strong intellect, of physical beauty, full at first of the joy of life, chivalrous, a believer in the innate goodness of human nature. Believing in goodness, he believed also ardently in influence. In fact, he was a worshipper of influence, and his main passion was to seize upon the personalities of others, and impose his own personality upon them. He loved to make men and women see with his eyes and hear with his ears, adopt his theories as truth, take his judgment for their own. All that he thought *was*—to him. He never doubted himself, therefore he could not bear that those around him should not think with him, act towards men and women as he acted, face life as he faced it. Yet he was too subtle ever to be dogmatic. He never shouted in the market-place. He led those with whom he came in contact as adroitly as if he had been evil, and to the influence of others he was as adamant.

Events brought into his life a woman, complex, subtle too, with a naturally noble character and fine understanding, a woman who, like so many women, might have been anything, and was far worse than nothing—a hopeless, helpless slave, the victim of the morphia habit, which had gradually degraded her, driven her through sloughs of immorality, wrecked a professional career which at one time had been almost great, shattered her constitution, though not all her still curious beauty, and ruined her, to all intents and purposes, body and soul. The man and the woman met, and in a flash the man saw what she had been, what she might have been, what, perhaps, in spite of all, she still was, somewhere, somehow. In her horrible degradation, in her dense despair, she fascinated him. He could only see the fire bursting out of the swamp. He could only feel on his cheek the breath of the spring in the darkness of the charnel-house. He knew that she gave to him his great lifework. Her monstrous habit he simply could not comprehend. It was altogether as fantastic to him as absolute virtue sometimes seems to absolute vice. He looked upon it, and felt as little kinship with it as a saint might feel with a vampire. To him it was merely a hideous and extraordinary growth, which had fastened like a cancer upon a beautiful and wonderful body, and which must be cut out. He was profoundly interested.

He loved the woman. Seeing her governed entirely by a vice, he made the very common mistake of believing her to have a weak personality, easily falling, perhaps for that very reason as easily lifted to her feet. He resolved to save her, to devote all his powers, all his subtlety, all his intellect, all his strong force of will, to weaning this woman from her fatal habit. She was a married woman, long ago left, to kill herself if she would, by the husband whose happiness she had wrecked. He took her to live with him. For her sake he defied the world, and set himself to do angel's work when people believed him at the devil's. He resolved to wrap her, to envelop her in his influence, to enclose her in his strong personality. Here, at last, was a grand, a noble opportunity for the legitimate exercise of his master passion. He was confident of victory.

But his faith in himself was misplaced. This woman, whom he thought so weak, was yet stronger than he. Although he could not influence her, he began to find that she could influence him. At first he struggled with her vice, which he could not understand. He thought himself merely horrified at it; then he began to lose the horror in wonder at its power. Its virility, as it were, fascinated him just a little. A vice so overwhelmingly strong seemed to him at length almost glorious, almost God-like. There was a sort of humanity about it. Yes, it was like a being who lived and who conquered.

The woman loved him, and he tried to win her from it; but her passion for it was greater than her passion for him, greater than had been her original passion for purity, for health, for success, for homage, for all lovely and happiness-making things. Her passion for it was so great that it roused the man's curiosity at last; it made him hold his breath, and stand in awe, and desire furtively to try just once for himself what its dominion was like, to test its power as one may test the power of an electric battery. He dared not do this openly, for fear the fact of his doing so might drive the woman still farther on the downward path. So in secret he tasted the fascinations of her vice, once—and again—and yet again. But still he struggled for her while he was ceasing to struggle for himself. Still he combated for her the foe who was conquering him. Very strange, very terrible was his position in that London house with her, isolated from the world. For his friends had dropped him. Even those who were not scandalized at his relations with this woman had ceased to come near him. They found him blind and deaf to the ordinary interests of life. He never went out anywhere, unless occasionally with her to some theatre. He never invited anyone to come and see him. At first the woman absorbed all his interest, all his powers of love—and then at last the woman and her vice, which was becoming his too. By degrees he sank lower and lower, but he never told the woman the truth, and he still urged her to give up her horrible habit, which now he loved. And she laughed in his face, and asked him if a human creature who had discovered a new life would be likely to give it up. "A new death," he murmured, and then, looking in a mirror near to him, saw his lips curved in the thin, pale smile of the hypocrite.

So far the two young men had written. They worked hard, but their industry was occasionally interrupted by the unaccountable laziness of Andrew, who, after toiling with unremitting fury for some days, and scarcely getting up from his desk, would disappear, and perhaps not return for several nights. Henley remonstrated with him, but in vain.

"But what do you do, my dear fellow?" he asked. "What becomes of you?"

"I go away to think out what is coming. The environment I seek helps me," answered Andrew, with a curious, gleaming smile. "I return full of fresh copy."

This was true enough. He generally mysteriously departed when the book was beginning to flag, and on his reappearance he always set to work with new vigour and confidence.

"It seems to me," Henley said, "that it will be your book after all, not mine. It is your plot, and when I think things over I find that every detail is yours. You insisted on the house where the man and the woman hid themselves being on the Chelsea Embankment. You invented the woman, her character, her appearance. You named her Olive Beauchamp."

"Olive Beauchamp," Andrew repeated, with a strange lingering over the two words, which he pronounced in a very curious voice that trembled, as if with some keen emotion, love or hate. "Yes; I named her as you say."

"Then, as the man in the play remarks, 'Where do I come in?'" Henley asked, half laughing, half vexed. "Upon my word, I shall have some compunction in putting my name below yours on the title-page when the book is published, if it ever is."

Andrew's lips twitched once or twice uneasily. Then he said, "You need not have any such compunction. The greatest chapter will probably be written by you."

"Which chapter do you mean?"

"That which winds the story up—that which brings the whole thing to its legitimate conclusion. You must write the *dénouement*."

"I doubt if I could. And then we have not even now decided what it is to be."

"We need not bother about that yet. It will come. Fate will decide it for us."

"What do you mean, Andrew? How curiously you talk about the book sometimes— so precisely as if it were true!"

Trenchard smiled again, struck a match, and lit his pipe.

"It seems true to me—when I am writing it," he answered. "I have been writing it these last two days and nights when I have been away, and now I can go forward, if you agree to the new development which I suggest."

It was night. He had been absent for some days, and had just returned. Henley, meanwhile, had been raging because the book had come to a complete standstill. He himself could do nothing at it, since they had reached a dead-lock, and had not talked over any new scenes, or mutually decided upon the turn events were now to take. He felt rather cross and sore.

"*You* can go forward," he said: "yes, after your holiday. You might at least tell me when you are going."

"I never know myself," Andrew said rather sadly.

He was looking very white and worn, and his eyes were heavy.

"But I have thought some fresh material out. My idea is this: The man now becomes such a complete slave to the morphia habit that concealment of the fact is scarcely possible. And, indeed, he ceases to desire to conceal it from the woman. The next scene will be an immensely powerful one—that in which he tells her the truth."

"You do not think it would be more natural if she found it out against his will? It seems to me that what he had concealed so long he would try to hide for ever."

"No," Andrew said emphatically; "that would not be so."

"But——"

"Look here," the other interrupted, with some obvious irritability; "let me tell you what I have conceived, and raise any objections afterwards if you wish to raise them. He would tell her the truth himself. He would almost glory in doing so. That is the nature of the man. We have depicted his pride in his own powers, his temptation, his struggle—his fall, as it would be called——"

"As it would be called."

"Well, well!—his fall, then. And now comes the moment when his fall is complete. He bends the neck finally beneath his tyrant, and then he goes to the woman and he tells her the truth."

"But explain matters a little more. Do you mean that he is glad, and tells almost with triumph; or that he is appalled, and tells her with horror?"

"Ah! That is where the power of the scene lies. He is appalled. He is like a man plunged at last into hell without hope of future redemption. He tells her the truth with horror."

"And she?"

"It is she who triumphs. Look here: it will be like this."

Andrew leaned forward across the table that stood between their two worn armchairs. His thin, feverish-looking hands, with the fingers strongly twisted together, rested upon it. His dark eyes glittered with excitement.

"It will be like this. It is evening—a dark, dull evening, like the day before yesterday, closing in early, throttling the afternoon prematurely, as it were. A drizzling rain falls softly, drenching everything—the sodden leaves of the trees on the Embankment, the road, which is heavy with clinging yellow mud, the stone coping of the wall that skirts the river.

"And the river heaves along. Its gray, dirty waves are beaten up by a light, chilly wind, and chase the black barges with a puny, fretful, sinister fury, falling back from their dark, wet sides with a hiss of baffled hatred. Yes, it is dreary weather.

"Do you know, Henley, as I know, the strange, subtle influence of certain kinds of weather? There are days on which I could do great deeds merely because of the way the sun is shining. There are days, there are evenings, when I could commit crimes merely because of the way the wind is whispering, the river is sighing, the dingy night is clustering around me. There can be an angel in the weather, or there can be a devil. On this evening I am describing there is a devil in the night!

"The lights twinkle through the drizzling rain, and they are blurred, as bright eyes are blurred, and made dull and ugly, by tears. Two or three cabs roll slowly by the houses on the Embankment.. A few people hurry past along the slippery, shining pavement. But as the night closes in there is little life outside those tall, gaunt houses that are so near the river! And in one of those houses the man comes down to the woman to tell her the truth.

"There is a devil in the weather that night, as I said, and that devil whispers to the man, and tells him that it is now his struggle must end finally, and the new era of unresisted yielding to the vice begin. In the sinister darkness, in the diminutive, drenching mist of rain, he speaks, and the man listens, and bows his head and answers 'yes!' It is over. He has fallen finally. He is resolved, with a strange, dull obstinacy that gives him a strange, dull pleasure—do you see?—to go down to the room below, and tell the woman that she has conquered him—that his power of will is a reed which can be crushed—that henceforth there shall be two victims instead of one. He goes down."

Andrew paused a moment. His lips were twitching again. He looked terribly excited. Henley listened in silence. He had lost all wish to interrupt.

"He goes down into the room below where the woman is, with her dark hair, and her dead-white face, and her extraordinary eyes—large, luminous, sometimes dull and without expression, sometimes dilated, and with an unnatural life staring out of them. She is on the sofa near the fire. He sits down beside her. His head falls into his hands, and at first he is silent. He is thinking how he will tell her. She puts her soft, dry hand on his, and she says: 'I am very tired to-night. Do not begin your evening sermon. Let me have it to-morrow. How you must love me to be so persistent! and how you must love me to be so stupid as to think that your power of will can break the power of such a habit as mine!'

"Then he draws his hand away from hers, and he lifts his head from his hands, and he tells her the truth. She leans back against a cushion staring at him in silence, devouring him with her eyes, which have become very bright and eager and searching. Presently he stops.

"'Go on,' she says, 'go on. Tell me more. Tell me all you feel. Tell me how the habit stole upon you, and came to you again and again, and stayed with you. Tell me how you first liked it, and then loved it, and how it was something to you, and then much, and then everything. Go on! go on!'

"And he catches her excitement. He conceals nothing from her. All the hideous, terrible, mental processes he has been through, he details to her, at first almost gloating over his own degradation. He even exaggerates, as a man exaggerates in telling a story to an eager auditor. He is carried away by her strange fury of listening. He lays bare his soul; he exposes its wounds; he sears them with red-hot irons for her to see. And then at last all is told. He can think of no more details. He has even embellished the abominable truth. So he is silent, and he looks at her."

"And what does she do?" asked Henley, with a catch in his voice as he spoke. Undoubtedly in relating a fictitious narrative Andrew had a quite abnormal power of making it appear true and real.

"She looks at him, and then she bursts out laughing. Her eyes shine with triumph. She is glad; she is joyous with the joy of a lost soul when it sees that other souls are irrevocably lost too; she laughs, and she says nothing."

"And the man?"

Andrew's eyes suddenly dilated. He leaned forward and laid his hand on Henley's arm.

"Ah, the man! that is my great idea. As she laughs his heart is changed. His love for her suddenly dies. Its place is taken by hatred. He realizes then, for the first time, while he hears her laugh, what she has done to him. He knows that she has ruined him, and that she is proud of it—that she is rejoicing in having won him to destruction. He sees that his perdition is merely a feather in her cap. He hates her. Oh, how he hates her!—hates her!"

The expression on Andrew's face became terrible as he spoke—cruel, malignant, almost fiendish. Henley turned cold, and shook off his hand abruptly.

"That is horrible!" he said. "I object to that. The book will be one of unrelieved gloom."

"The book!" said Andrew.

"Yes. You behave really as if the story were true, as if everything in it were ordained—inevitable."

"It seems so to me; it is so. What must be, must be. If you are afraid of tragedy, you ought never to have joined me in starting upon such a story. Even what has never happened must be made to seem actual to be successful. The art of fiction is to imitate truth with absolute fidelity, not to travesty it. In such circumstances the man's love would be changed to hatred."

"Yes, if the woman's demeanour were such as you have described. But why should she be so callous? I do not think that is natural."

"You do not know the woman," began Andrew harshly. Then he stopped speaking abruptly, and a violent flush swept over his face.

"I know her as well as you do, my dear fellow," rejoined Henley, laughing. "How you manage to live in your dreams! You certainly do create an atmosphere for yourself with a vengeance, and for me too. I believe you have an abnormal quantity of electricity concealed about you somewhere, and sometimes you give me a shock and carry me out of myself. If this is collaboration, it is really a farce. From the very first you have had things all your own way. You have talked me over to your view upon every single occasion; but now I am going to strike. I object to the conduct you have devised for Olive. It will alienate all sympathy from her; it is the behaviour of a devil."

"It is the behaviour of a woman," said Andrew, with a cold cynicism that seemed to cut like a knife.

"How can you tell? How can you judge of women so surely?"

"I study all strange phenomena, women among the rest."

"Have you ever met an Olive Beauchamp, then, in real life?" said Henley.

The question was put more than half in jest; but Trenchard received it with a heavy frown.

"Don't let us quarrel about the matter," he said, "I can only tell you this; and mind, Jack, I mean it. It is my unalterable resolve. Either the story must proceed upon the lines that I have indicated, or I cannot go on with it at all. It would be impossible for me to write it differently."

"And this is collaboration, is it?" exclaimed the other, trying to force a laugh, though even his good-nature could scarcely stand Trenchard's trampling demeanour.

"I can't help it. I cannot be inartistic and untrue to Nature even for the sake of a friend."

"Thank you. Well, I have no desire to ruin your work, Andrew; but it is really useless for this farce to continue. Do what you like, and let us make no further pretence of collaborating. I cannot act as a drag upon such a wheel as yours. I will not any longer be a dead-weight upon you. Our temperaments evidently unfit us to be fellow-workers; and I feel that your strength and power are so undeniable that you may, perhaps, be able to carry this weary tragedy through, and by sheer force make it palatable to the public. I will protest no more; I will only cease any longer to pretend to have a finger in this literary pie."

Andrew's morose expression passed away like a cloud. He got up and laid his hand upon Henley's shoulder.

"You make me feel what a beast I am," he said. "But I can't help it. I was made so. Do forgive me, Jack. I have taken the bit between my teeth, I know. But—this story seems to me no fiction; it is a piece of life, as real to me as those stars I see through the window-pane are real to me—as my own emotions are real to me. Jack, this book has seized me. Believe me, if it is written as I wish, it will make an impression upon the world that will be great. The mind of the world is given to me like a sheet of blank paper. I will write upon it with my heart's blood. But"—and here his manner became strangely impressive, and his sombre, heavy eyes gazed deeply into the eyes of his friend—"remember this! You will finish this book. I feel that; I know it. I cannot tell you why. But so it is ordained. Let me write as far as I can, Jack, and let me write as I will. But do not let us quarrel. The book is ours, not mine. And—don't—don't take away your friendship from me."

The last words were said with an outburst of emotion that was almost feminine in intensity. Henley felt deeply moved, for, as a rule, Andrew's manner was not specially affectionate, or even agreeable.

"It is all right, old fellow," he said, in the embarrassed English manner which often covers so much that might with advantage be occasionally revealed. "Go on in your own way. I believe you are a genius, and I am only trying to clip the wings that may carry you through the skies. Go on in your own way, and consult me only when you feel inclined."

Andrew took his hand and pressed it in silence.

III.

It was some three weeks after this that one afternoon Trenchard laid down his pen at the conclusion of a chapter, and, getting up, thrust his hands into his pockets and walked to the window.

The look-out was rather dreary. A gray sky leaned over the great, barrack-like church that gives an ecclesiastical flavour to Smith's Square. A few dirty sparrows fluttered above the gray pavement—feverish, unresting birds, Trenchard named them silently, as he watched their meaningless activity, their jerky, ostentatious deportment, with lacklustre, yet excited, eyes. How gray everything looked, tame, colourless, indifferent! The light was beginning to fade stealthily out of things. The gray church was gradually becoming shadowy. The flying forms of the hurrying sparrows disappeared in the weary abysses of the air and sky. The sitting-room in Smith's Square was nearly dark now. Henley had gone out to a *matinée* at one of the theatres, so Trenchard was alone. He struck a match presently, lit a candle, carried it over to his writing-table, and began to examine the littered sheets he had just been writing. The book was nearing its end. The tragedy was narrowing to a point. Trenchard read the last paragraph which he had written:

"He hardly knew that he lived, except during those many hours when, plunged in dreams, he allowed, nay, forced, life to leave him for awhile. He had sunk to depths below even those which Olive had reached. And the thought that she was ever so little above him haunted him like a spectre impelling him to some mysterious deed. When he was not dreaming, he was dwelling upon this idea which had taken his soul captive. It seemed to be shaping itself towards an act. Thought was the ante-room through which he passed to the hall where Fate was sitting, ready to give him audience. He traversed this ante-room, which seemed lined with fantastic and terrible pictures, at first with lagging footfalls. But at length he laid his hand upon the door that divided him from Fate."

And when he had read the final words he gathered the loose sheets together with his long, thin fingers, and placed them one on the top of the other in a neat pile. He put them into a drawer which contained other unfinished manuscripts, shut the drawer, locked it, and carried the key to Henley's room. There he scribbled some words on a bit of notepaper, wrapped the key in it, and inclosed it in an envelope on which he wrote Henley's name. Then he put on his overcoat, descended the narrow stairs, and opened the front-door. The landlady heard him, and screamed from the basement to know if he would be in to dinner.

"I shall not be in at all to-night," he answered, in a hard, dry voice that travelled along the dingy passage with a penetrating distinctness. The landlady murmured to the slatternly maidservant an ejaculatory diatribe on the dissipatedness of young literary gentlemen as the door banged. Trenchard disappeared in the gathering darkness, and soon left Smith's Square behind him.

It chanced that day that, in the theatre, Henley encountered some ladies who carried him home to tea after the performance. They lived in Chelsea, and in returning to Smith's Square afterwards Henley took his way along the Chelsea Embankment. He always walked near to the dingy river when he could. The contrast of its life to the town's life through which it flowed had a perpetual fascination for him. In the early evening, too, the river presents many Doré effects. It is dim, mysterious, sometimes meretricious, with its streaks of light close to the dense shadows that lie under the bridges, its wailful, small waves licking the wharves, and bearing up the inky barges that look like the ferry-boat of the Styx. Henley loved to feel vivaciously despairing, and he hugged himself in the belief that the Thames at nightfall tinged his soul with a luxurious melancholy, the capacity for which was not far from rendering him a poet. So he took his way by the river. As he neared Cheyne Row, he saw in front of him the figure of a man leaning over the low stone wall, with his face buried in his hands. On hearing his approaching footsteps the man lifted himself up, turned round, and preceded him along the pavement with a sort of listless stride which seemed to Henley strangely familiar. He hastened his steps, and on coming closer recognised that the man was Trenchard; but, just as he was about to hail him, Trenchard crossed the road to one of the houses opposite, inserted a key in the door, and disappeared within, shutting the door behind him.

Henley paused a moment opposite to the house. It was of a dull red colour, and had a few creepers straggling helplessly about it, looking like a torn veil that can only partially conceal a dull, heavy face.

"Andrew seems at home here," he thought, gazing up at the blind, tall windows, which showed no ray of light. "I wonder——"

And then, still gazing at the windows, he recalled the description of the house where Olive Beauchamp lived in their book.

"He took it from this," Henley said to himself. Yes, that was obvious. Trenchard had described the prison-house of despair, where the two victims of a strange, desolating habit shut themselves up to sink, with a curious minuteness. He had even devoted a paragraph to the tall iron gate, whose round handle he had written of as "bald, and exposed to the wind from the river, the paint having long since been worn off it." In the twilight Henley bent down and examined the handle of the gate. The paint seemed to have been scraped from it.

"How curiously real that book has become to me!" he muttered. "I could almost believe that if I knocked upon that door, and was let in, I should find Olive Beauchamp stretched on a couch in the room that lies beyond those gaunt, shuttered windows."

He gave a last glance at the house, and as he did so he fancied that he heard a slight cry come from it to him. He listened attentively and heard nothing more. Then he walked away toward home.

When he reached his room, he found upon his table the envelope which Trenchard had directed to him. He opened it, and unwrapped the key from the inclosed sheet of note-paper, on which were written these words:

"Dear Jack,

"I am off again. And this time I can't say when I shall be

back. In any case, I have completed my part of the book, and

leave the finishing of it in your hands. This is the key of

the drawer in which I have locked the manuscript. You have

not seen most of the last volume. Read it, and judge for

yourself whether the dénouement can be anything but

utterly tragic. I will not outline to you what I have

thought of for it. If you have any difficulty about the

finale, I shall be able to help you with it even if you do

not see me again for some time. By the way, what nonsense

that saying is, 'Dead men tell no tales!' Half the best

tales in the world are told, or at least completed, by dead

men.

"Yours ever,

"A. T."

Henley laid this note down and turned cold all over. It was the concluding sentence which had struck a chill through his heart. He took the key in his hand, went down to Trenchard's room, unlocked the drawer in his writing-table, and took out the manuscript. What did Andrew mean by that sinister sentence? A tale completed by a dead man! Henley sat down by the fire with the manuscript in his hands and began to read. He was called away to dinner; but immediately afterward he returned to his task, and till late into the night his glance travelled down the closely-written sheets one after the other, until the light from the candles grew blurred and indistinct, and his eyes ached. But still he read on. The power and gloom of Andrew's narrative held him in a vice, and then he was searching for a clue in the labyrinth of words. At last he came to the final paragraph, and then to the final sentence:

"But at length he laid his hand upon the door that divided him from Fate."

Henley put the sheet down carefully upon the table. It was three o'clock in the morning, and the room seemed full of a strange, breathless cold, the peculiar chilliness that precedes the dawn. The fire was burning brightly enough, yet the warmth it emitted scarcely seemed to combat the frosty air that penetrated from without, and Henley shivered as he rose from his seat. His brows were drawn together, and he was thinking deeply. A light seemed slowly struggling into his soul. That last sentence of Tren-chard's connected itself with what he had seen in the afternoon on the Chelsea Embankment. "He laid his hand upon the door that divided him from Fate."

A strange idea dawned in Henley's mind, an idea which made many things clear to him. Yet he put it away, and sat down again to read the unfinished book once more. Andrew had carried on the story of the man's growing hatred of the woman whom he had tried to rescue, until it had developed into a deadly fury, threatening immediate action. Then he had left the *dénouement* in Henley's hands. He had left it ostensibly in Henley's hands, but the latter, reading the manuscript again with intense care, saw that matters had been so contrived that the knot of the novel could only be cut by murder. As it had been written, the man must inevitably murder the woman. And Andrew? All through the night Henley thought of him as he had last seen him, opening the door of the red house with the tattered creepers climbing over it.

At last, when it was dawn, he went up to bed tired out, after leaving a written direction to the servant not to call him in the morning. When he awoke and looked at his watch it was past two o'clock in the afternoon. He sprang out of bed, dressed, and after a hasty meal, half breakfast, half lunch, set out towards Chelsea. The day was bright and cold. The sun shone on the river and sparkled on the windows of the houses on the Embankment. Many people were about, and they looked cheerful. The weight of depression that had settled upon Henley was lifted. He thought of the strange, yet illuminating, idea that had occurred to him in the night, and now, in broad daylight, it seemed clothed in absurdity. He laughed at it. Yet he quickened his steps toward the red house with the tarnished iron gate and the tattered creepers.

But long before he reached it he met a boy sauntering along the thoroughfare and shouting newspapers. He sang out unflinchingly in the gay sunshine, "Murder! Murder!" and between his shouts he whistled a music-hall song gaily in snatches. Henley stopped him and bought a paper. He opened the paper in the wind, which seemed striving to prevent him, and cast his eyes over the middle pages. Then suddenly he dropped it to the ground with a white face, and falteringly signed to a cabman. The *dénouement* was written. The previous night, in a house on the Chelsea Embankment, a woman had been done to death, and the murderer had crept out and thrown himself into the gray, hurrying river.

The woman's name was Olive Beauchamp.

End of the book.